"Build It On Passion is great for the genuine reader. It helps you distinguish between your wants, loves, and passions. What makes it unique is that those who are looking for their passion in life will definitely find it by reading this book. It will help you stay motivated and give you a reason to keep on going. You can feel Tony's passion throughout the book for helping others find their own!"

- Mark Duvall, Retail Manager / Teacher

BUILD "IT" ON PASSION

First edition. Published in paperback in the United States by Nevaeh Marketing, LLC in 2009.

ISBN 13: 978-0-615-32755-6

www.builditonpassion.com
builditonpassion@hotmail.com

This edition designed and typeset by HailesArt LLC
www.hailesart.com

Printed in the U.S.A.

10 9 8 7 6 5 4 3 2 1

Acknowledgments

Dedication to:

My wife and daughter for the support they have given me, for the additional help and words of advice to keep me on track. Having them in my life gives me endless strength.

Special thanks to:

Mark Duvall for taking time out of his busy life to edit this book. He did an incredible job supporting me and showing me tough love. I couldn't have finished this book without him.

My family and friends, I love each and every one of you. I am grateful for your influence and most important to have you all in my life.

Last, to my Creator who has given me this beautiful world and the ability to see life, live life, and to experience passion every day.

BUILD "IT" ON PASSION

Discover your passions, live life
with passion and find success
through the 6 step Passion Cycle

Tony P. Glick

Nevaeh Marketing, LLC

Contents

Chapter 1

Passion

Live life without fear and with unshakable passion.

Living Life with Passion

Thank you for opening this book.

I want to introduce myself before you begin reading. Whether you know me or not, I think it is important that you understand who I am and why I have spent much time and energy writing this book. First of all, I want you to know that my intentions are pure and honest, and what you will read comes straight from my heart. It has been fun and challenging as I have taken my mind and abilities to a whole new level. I have discovered through writing this book that the mind is a powerful tool, and inside all of us there is a story.

I am currently pursuing and living many dreams in my life. I have a beautiful wife, a healthy

and happy daughter, I own part of two grow-
ing companies, and I am a happy, carefree individual. My one desire is to share with people
my passion for life and help them pursue their
own, unique passion.

Life is about taking risks, living your dreams,
accepting challenges and trying to do that
which seems impossible to others. I love life,
and I have come to understand that we all have
to accept and pursue different paths in order to
find complete happiness. Passion has gotten
me where I am today. I am a very normal person, living a normal life with a powerful message that can take your life to a new level as it
has mine.

As you continue reading and ultimately discover your own passions, it's not just a matter
of stepping foot on the path; it's about applying
powerful principles and a process to the path.
This book will help you discover your passions
and also provide a proven process that will help
you apply passion every step of the way.

Again thank you for opening this book and best
of luck on whatever journey this takes you.

You can achieve whatever you want to in this
life, if you apply passion and put your mind
to it.

Building "IT"

To help you understand the overall function of this book, I want to explain the layout of all 12 chapters so you can keep your mind organized and focused on the overall message. Inside each chapter you will find sub chapters. Each sub chapter has one of my own personal quotes that are directly related to the topic. The sub chapters are simple, powerful and concise paragraphs filled with personal stories and motivational ideas on the subject. Any time in this book there is a reference to "IT", I am talking about your passions, goals, dreams and desires.

The book is split into three sections. Chapters 1 through 4 are focused primarily on the principle of passion. You will learn how passion can positively affect your goals, dreams, success and overall happiness in this life. These chapters will also serve as a thinking pad as you prepare your mind toward the many paths you wish to pursue. My hope is that after the beginning chapters you will have a greater love for yourself, and more importantly that you will understand how passion can influence your life in a powerful way.

Chapter 5 has a visual image of the passion cycle, and will explain the everyday purpose it holds day-to-day in your personal life.

Chapters 6 through 12 will cover in detail the Passion Cycle. Like any house that is constructed, if there is no foundation it would eventually crumble. The same goes for any goal you have in life. Therefore, the last chapters of this book will focus on the six principles inside the Passion Cycle. Anytime in your life that you have something important you want to accomplish or build these principles will serve as a foundation. I promise if you utilize these six principles on a daily basis, the power of passion will be fully ingrained in your soul, and you will find excitement with any journey you choose to pursue.

Last, remember we live in a world hungry and thirsty for happiness. I have no doubt that you can find complete happiness if you apply genuine passion in your own life.

Chapter 2

Discovering Your Passion

A prosperous life is lived through pursuing your own path, not chasing after the dreams and goals of other people.

Your Path

Each sub-chapter inside "Discover Your Passion" is intended to get your mind thinking and eventually committing to the path you wish to pursue. Success and happiness in this life is found by following your passions.

Have you stepped foot on your path?

I want you to remember that there are multiple paths and many directions that our dreams can take us. The key to life is understanding, finding and creating a path upon which you would then have the courage to step foot towards. In most of our lives we have many dreams, desires and goals. My hope is that this message will encourage you to think, learn and apply passion in the important areas of your life that you are pursuing or wish to pursue.

Someone once told me as I was discussing with her the power of passion, that she didn't know what her path was nor did she believe that if she found it, she could apply passion to it. I thought about this person and this conversation for some time, and I came to realize that we are all at different levels in life and that this was not an uncommon thought. However, whether you are currently pursuing something or not, remember that we are given infinite potential in this life to do whatever we want to do, and to be whoever we want to be! It's ours to take! That's the beauty of living!

Commitment is a fundamental key to success.
If you skip that step you will never be able to
draw enough courage to finish what you have
started.

Commitment

Before you move on, I want you to take a minute and answer these questions:

Do you have challenges in front of you?

Do you feel lost at times?

Are you trying to achieve something important?

Do you want to be better at something?

Do you hate going to work?

Do you want to make more money?

Do you want to improve your relationships?

Do you lack passion?

If you answered 'yes' to any of these questions, I have ideas within this book and chapter that will get you moving in a positive direction. However, first I need you to commit to yourself that you will be open to a new set of principles. You might ask yourself, why? Because the principles you will learn in this book cannot be utilized to it's fullest without a 100% commitment.

*By acknowledging the small successes of life,
you prepare yourself for giant challenges, and
most importantly you give yourself the opportunity to succeed.*

Success & Happiness

Now let's talk about success and happiness for a minute.

I am tired of hearing people measure success and happiness by the dollar amount they put into their account. Aren't you? Don't get me wrong; monetary success is a huge part of the success handbook. However, how much money you have is not and will never be the key component to happiness.

We all know that a part of happiness comes from success. So I'll ask you an important question: What defines your success?

Let's take a young couple for example who have spent years courting, having fun and getting to know one another. The big day comes in which they decide to get married. They take months to plan for the perfect wedding and finally the day comes that they stand across from each other at the wedding ceremony. At the ceremony, they commit to be faithful to each other, and to serve and honor one another. Then, the big question is asked. They both take a deep breath and say, 'I do.' Seconds later, they follow up with a spicy kiss to seal the deal! Now, is this happiness? It better be! Is this success? Absolutely! Success is measured in countless ways.

Unfortunately, the world has blocked out the simple successes of life and has placed too much emphasis on the larger, obvious successes. These days, we seem to be focused, generally speaking, on the giant successes in life; our bank account, the house we live in, the car we drive and so forth. Focusing on these successes is both exciting and challenging! However, the point is this: it's the continuous realization of the simple triumphs-the small things-that fuel our passion to achieve the giant successes.

Chapter 3

Passion Defined

Our world is full of passion; are you contributing?

Your Contribution

Chapter three is designed to do a few things. First: To help you understand who you are and how your passion can affect the people around you. Second: We will discuss the power of passion. And third: Why passion is an essential fuel for your body.

Ask yourself honestly: Are you contributing to this life in the way that you want to? If you have trouble answering this question, a great question to ask yourself is this: What am I doing on a daily basis to make this world and the people who surround me better?

We are all placed on this earth with a unique mission. I want you to understand how important you are to this world, to this country and to your individual community. Find the time and learn how to contribute in your own special way. By paying attention to how you can affect the people who surround you, your life will be more rewarding, and you will find success in every stride. And most importantly, your passion will spread to those whom surround you.

The burning desire within you, driving you toward success, that is passion.

What is Passion?

I recognized years ago, when I deliberately implemented passion on a certain goal, that it was an obvious tool for success. In my life, I have leaned continuously on the power of passion, and I have also learned countless lessons and have been fortunate enough to be in a position to share my ideas in many ways. Through training sessions I have held on this topic and much thought, I have compiled my own definitions in regards to what passion is, how to identify it, and how to use it.

Passion is belief, love, fire, desire, will, determination, charisma, vision and focus. Passion is the "starting line" and the "root" of all success. It is the fire in your eyes, the persuasion in your voice, and your body language when you walk. Passion is the power and foundation behind all human success. When I talk about passion I believe it is what makes the world go round. Without passion, our world would be very gloomy and slow. Just as a drop of water can cause a ripple that expands, likewise, a single drop of passion used in the right way produces more energy, optimism, smiles and successful people. The beauty of passion is that we can all obtain this powerful gift and utilize it to our advantage in our own unique way.

Passion enables us to see the world as a place of infinite potential. For example, a passionate person would see a dark and gloomy day as an opening to create light and opportunity; whereas the person with no passion may see the day as it is and would miss the potential the world has provided. With passion you also get that feeling of invincibility or endless ability and wonderment. Don't ever forget that! Passionate people are always looking for opportunities. I believe that passion is a gift that can spread to everyone and those that can gain a deeper love of it, and learn to use it, will ultimately find happiness and success in their lifetime.

The world needs people who are alive and moving. Find out what makes you come alive and do something about it.

The Living Fuel

I was at the local gas station one morning filling up my vehicle when I realized that it cost me $10 more than it did a few months ago. What's discouraging is that I also realized that the price of gasoline is out of my control so I'll continue to pay because the bottom line is that cars can't run without gas!

Passion is essentially the fuel our body and mind need to run. The beautiful thing is that this fuel doesn't cost a dime!

One way you can distinguish if you are failing to fuel your body with passion is to identify in your life where you lack the implementation of passion. Ask yourself these questions honestly:

Do I enjoy work?

Do I enjoy life?

Am I a happy person?

Do people like to be around me?

Do I like to wake up in the morning?

In general, am I optimistic?

It's important that you learn how to take the time daily and weekly to fuel your body with passion. Unlike a Chevy or BMW, your body can still move without fuel. However, without the constant fuel of passion you could find yourself thousands of steps behind others always trying to catch up. Even though you move physically, you will not be moving passionately. Moving without passion is what causes people to run out of gas, fall into ruts, and ultimately holds them back from coming alive.

Our bodies need fuel! I have two simple refueling tips to help you on a daily basis.

1. At night before you go to bed, think of something simple that excites you to wake up the next day. As simple as this exercise sounds, I promise it will change your outlook everyday and you will wake up refueled with passion.

For example, one night my wife and I went grocery shopping. As we walked through the cereal isle she reached down and picked up a box of Captain Crunch®. I thought to myself, 'perfect choice.' I was very tempted when we got home to crack open that box of cereal, but it was late so I decided not to eat it that night. Once that decision was made, I immediately planned for tomorrow. That Captain Crunch® was my choice of cereal in the morning and as silly as it sounds, I had a renewed excitement to wake up in the morning. I have no doubt that it is the little things that refuel our body full of passion each day; it's the simple things that excite us to wake each morning. It could be anything! Your favorite cereal, your wife, a child, a meeting, a co-worker, a football game, basketball, a play, a concert, a new pair of pants, Friday, a song, some sunshine, the snow, or even the rain. Whatever it is, there is no wrong answer. Go to bed each and every night eager to wake up the next day.

2. Find a day where you can refuel the passion and energy toward your long term goals. I usually find that the best day for me to refuel is Sunday before the week starts. I have used this day for years, and ironically Monday has become my favorite day of the week. This is a habit that has stuck with me for years. There is so much power behind this concept because it prepares you for things to come, and keeps you focused and passionate on the goals you are trying to accomplish.

Chapter 4

Lead with Passion

Leaders carve the path.

Be a Leader

All leaders are passionate people in one way or another. This chapter is intended to bring out the leader inside of you, which in turn will ignite the passion inside of you.

Over the years, I have found that leadership qualities are necessary for everyone. Those that cultivate leadership qualities and build upon them will be maturely prepared to handle any given situation. So, I have written this chapter to help you understand your personal leadership behaviors. You will find that my definition of a leader is not always someone who stands out in front of the crowd because I believe some of the greatest leaders are the quiet ones who are behind the scenes. What makes these definitions so special is that you will learn that each leadership skill you possess will help you in some form in this life when pursuing your passions.

Why practice being a leader?

Our world is run by leaders; it doesn't matter the capacity, company, or situation. I have never been part of any successful organization that doesn't have good leadership. Learn and identify what type of leader you are and master that skill so you are able to utilize it in whatever situation you find yourself in throughout this life. Know that every skill you learn is transferable into anything else you do.

Discover who you are as a leader, then find an effective way to influence the people who surround you.

Leadership Test

Back at a time when I ran a very large sales floor, I had six extremely opinionated, dedicated and gifted managers. They were all fun to work around and more importantly, they were all hungry for success. Now, my job was to not only help them and their teams make money, but, also to figure out the best way possible I could utilize each unique talent to build a successful sales floor. This was so important because I knew that as the leader of this group, if I could understand them personally, I could create a more powerful organization by using their skills correctly. Ultimately, with this knowledge I was able to create more success and keep order in an office full of 60 wild and crazy sales people.

As a result, I came up with this test. First, I created my own definitions that described 4 types of leaders. Then I asked each manager to identify the two leadership types they bore a resemblance to and the two leadership types they would like to work on. After they had done that, I asked them to fortify the two types they felt strong in and improve the other two types they desired to improve. I also had them write down ways they could impact the office with their personal leadership skills.

The results were absolutely amazing! I found that by doing this exercise my managers became more passionate in their personal lives and, most importantly, I watched as each manager utilized their passion for life to become a more genuine and fearless leader around the office.

I want you to go through this same exercise. Below are the four types of leaders I identified for my sales team. Try to recognize the two areas that best resemble you, and the two that you can improve on.

4 Types of Leaders

1. Movers – These leaders are not afraid to break and follow rules. They stand up for what is right. They will cut against the grain even if it's not popular. They have no fear; and they are pure winners! You can "feel" the confidence and strength in these leaders.

2. Shakers – These leaders are innovative; they love to think outside the box. They are creative, they are problem solvers and everyone expects them to do the unexpected. They shake things up and are not afraid to fail! They are the ones that most consider "extreme"! They live on the edge and take chances.

3. Motivators – These leaders are inspiring. They use life's experience to grow. They are great listeners, learners and teachers. They find joy in reaching out to everyone! The thought of connecting, teaching and inspiring someone to be better is their mission in life. You are empowered by their presence.

4. Lovers – These leaders are sympathetic and great listeners. They are honest, they have in-

tegrity, and they are intuitive people. Everyone loves to be around them. They make you feel good. They are trustworthy and loyal. These are the genuine, "quiet" leaders that people sincerely enjoy to follow.

Did you recognize the two leadership areas that you best resemble? Great! Now remember like I mentioned in the early chapters your potential is infinite, and your ability to be who you want to be is great. So, now that you have recognized the two that you resemble, take the other two and with them learn, practice and add upon your abilities. I promise by doing this exercise, and by living up to your leadership abilities, the passion inside of you will be contagious, and the people whom you lead will never let you down.

Chapter 5

The Passion Cycle

*A thriving system that can be repeated over
and over again is the key to constant success.*

Turn Key

I developed the Passion Cycle around the
Turnkey concept. The definition of Turnkey
is "something ready for use." What a simple
and brilliant concept! For example, if I were
to give you the keys to my car, and ask you to
start the engine, when you turn the key the engine should start up on its own, right? Now, in
order to make the car move, all I need is someone with a license that can drive. The same
principle is applied in the Passion Cycle. The
Passion Cycle serves as the engine for any goal
you have in life; all you need to do is imple-
ment the six principles on a specific goal and
then drive.

I have used this concept and these principles
over and over in my life and have seen how

the Passion Cycle is the key to continual success. The Passion Cycle is easy to follow; it is
proven to work "and ready for use."

The Passion Cycle

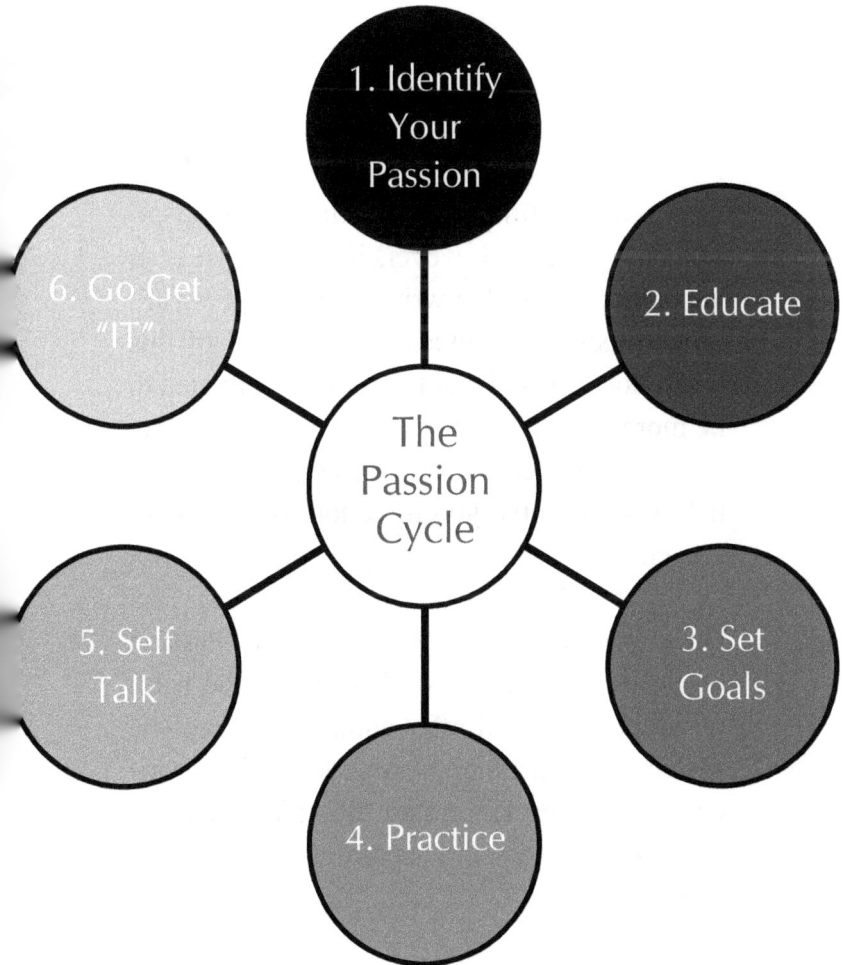

1. Identify
Your
Passion

6. Go Get
"IT"

2. Educate

The
Passion
Cycle

5. Self
Talk

3. Set
Goals

4. Practice

Habit allows us to not only achieve greatness
but to be great over and over again.

Habit

This book is full of motivational and inspirational quotes. However, if that's all it is to you, my purpose for writing this book wasn't accomplished. Ultimately, at the end of this book, not only do I want you to be motivated to be more passionate, but I want you to feel like you have gained six new principles that will help you and give you direction for each path you chose to pursue.

Once you learn how to employ the Passion Cycle in specific areas of your life, the habit of adding one goal after another will become systematic. In other words, you will experience a transformation and this transformation will breed success and happiness in all areas of your life.

Chapter 6

Identify Your Passions

Desire is what wakes us up in the morning and is the starting point for turning dreams into reality.

Be Clear and Specific

Are you ready to get started with the Passion Cycle? Identifying your Passions is the first step in the Passion Cycle. So to help us get started, I want you to ask yourself a question.

What is the most important goal in my life?

What I want you to do now is to take a minute and think about some other goals and desires that you have in your life. As mentioned in the earlier section, I don't want you to overwhelm yourself with too much so try to narrow these down to the ones that are the most important. They can be either long-term or short-term desires. What's important is that these desires are the most important ones in your life. For example, a short-term desire could be writing a book, getting an A on an exam, or finishing an important work project. Some long-term desires could be building a successful marriage, saving for a house, or even travel to Europe. This is the most important part of the book, so take sufficient time to think. Like I talked about at the beginning of the book, this is your opportunity to decide what the specific dreams, or passions, are that you want to follow.

Write your desires in this book, on a piece of paper, or cvcn carvc it into a tree! Wherever you choose to write your desires, make sure you place them somewhere you can see them daily.

Next, share your goals with someone close to you. The reason why you want to share your goals with someone close is to have accountability and, more importantly, to allow people to have a part in your dreams.

*Identify your passion and then with patience-
live it.*

Balance and Manage

The process of using passion is a lifetime commitment, and if used correctly, this process can
and will empower you constantly as you attempt to take your life to a higher level. Now,
it's important not to become overwhelmed, so
part of this process is to understand how to balance and manage your passions.

I want you to think of the words 'balance and
manage' for a minute. The word balance is defined as "a state of equilibrium" and the word
manage is defined as" to be in charge."

So, when it comes to important goals in your
life, how often do you feel unbalanced and not
in charge? If you said often, you're not alone.
I think it is very common for people to want to

do more and in some cases, too much. This desire to do more creates a lack of structure, focus and clear direction in people's lives..

So again, the key is learning how to balance and manage the "busyness" of your daily life by not adding too much. If you are unable to grasp onto this concept, you may never be able to exert the energy and passion necessary to accomplish what is really important to you, and ultimately, impede your progress toward your goals. So remember, the first step is to understand those two words "balance and Manage" and the second step is deciding what's important as you identify your Passions.

Chapter 7

Educate

Education on any level increases confidence, opportunity, and the ability to accomplish any goal that is placed in front of you.

The Power of Education

Educating yourself is the second step in the Passion Cycle. Education, when used properly, will serve as a launching pad, and mentally will give you a boost of confidence on every journey.

Educating yourself can be, with out a doubt, one of the hardest things to do. Personally, I have never liked to study on any level. Although this is the most difficult step for me, it is one of the most important principles of the cycle. After making a decision to move forward on a desired path, understand that every path requires deep education.

Our minds can absorb substantial information no matter who we are or where we come from.

One of the greatest benefits we have today is we have access to endless information. Just about anything we want to know is at our fingertips! Now, in order to complete the highest level of success with anything you do, you must have the discipline to always take the time to educate yourself before you take any steps forward.

Some of the greatest education you will receive in this lifetime comes from observing those who surround you.

People Watch

Have you ever sat down in the middle of a crowded area and watched the people around you in conversation? Isn't it fun?

Some of the greatest education I have received in my life has come from watching, listening and observing people. I love it! I have learned to observe all people and to take the good, the bad and the ugly; and then learn from what I observe and use it in my own life. I would be lost without all of you.

A while back as I was walking into the local gym, I noticed two gym employees outside in a heated argument. Not trying to interrupt the argument, I decided to take a seat on the curb next to the two gym employees and listen to their argument. Immediately, I recognized that one of them was older and most likely the manager and the other guy was quite a bit younger and most likely one of his employees.

As the argument continued, I learned that they were both salesmen, and that the younger gentleman felt that the distribution of leads was unfair and that it was affecting his ability to make sales. At one point the younger salesman was furious and almost punched the manager in the face. In fact, he actually motioned a couple of swings to try and intimidate the manager.

After a while they both calmed down and the confrontation came to a close; unresolved but closed for the time being. As they went their ways, the younger fellow remained outside pacing back and forth talking to himself in anger. I sat and continued to watch the free entertainment. After a while he turned right at me and realized what I was doing. He stared at me and began to walk toward me. I stood up and prepared for the worst! As he approached, he looked right at me and said, "I noticed you were watching and I apologize for using foul language."

We sat and chatted for the next little while about his situation, and the frustration he was feeling. At one point I asked him if he enjoyed sales. He confidently replied by saying, "I'm good at it, and I make good money, so yes." That response brought a smile to my face, and I agreed with him and told him I could tell he was talented. I thought to myself as I walked away that if that kid could manage his passion and his emotion in the heat of battle he would be a great friend, employee and a much better salesman.

That experience was significant later on that day as I found myself in a heated discussion with a good friend of mine. In the middle of the discussion, I thought of the young salesman I met earlier that day. As my emotions were starting to increase, I felt myself wanting to re-act in a similar way as the salesman. I realized that I too get personally caught in the same trap in the heat of battle. This experience reminded me of the importance of controlling my emotions when involved in a disagreement. Also, it reminded me how important it is to continue learning from the people around me.

We have 24 hours in a day . . . pace yourself and learn.

Student for Life

Why take the time to learn? Why be a life student? Consider this: have you ever held off studying for an important test? How did you do on the test the next day?

When I was in school, I was in this situation many times and without fail I would attempt to take tests thinking I was smart enough 'just to get by.' I don't know where I got that idea from because every time I went to take a test it seemed foreign and unfamiliar and even though I knew better, I would still take that chance over and over again.

The same process goes for life decisions, goals, and challenges. The more prepared and educated we are, the better chance we have to pass.

You are never too far behind as long as you take the time.

When faced with new goals, how often do you take sufficient time to educate yourself?

My point is this: learn to be a student for life and don't stop learning! I will mention this again in the upcoming chapters because what the world needs in order to progress is experts and intelligent people. The more experts we have, the better and more skilled the world will get, and you will be more prepared to confront any challenge or goal in front of you.

Before you step foot on any path, know what you are doing, how to do it, and most importantly, be committed.

Step Forward

Many times when I am in a hurry to get up the stairs in my house, I instinctively take the first step up without looking. I think that is pretty normal. However, on occasion, I miss that first step and either stub my toe or twist my ankle. Can you relate? If so, I feel your pain! Many times in life we go through stumbling, and even painful experiences like this when we take our first step toward a goal without proper education. You can eliminate this experience by spending adequate time educating yourself.

I have purposely placed this sub-chapter last under the education process because I believe that once you have identified a specific desire in your life, and you have spent sufficient time educating yourself, that you are ready for success. The phrase step forward is a commitment to yourself to move forward and never to look back. The time you spend learning will give you the confidence, clear vision and courage you need to step forward.

I promise if you follow this principle with real intent that stepping forward will seem easy, and your commitment toward a specific goal will be unbreakable.

Chapter 8

Set
Goals

Goal setting is a powerful process, and creates the discipline necessary to start turning vision into reality.

Goals = Clear Vision

Setting Goals is the third step in the Passion Cycle. This step is so extremely important. The process of writing down goals provides a road map on your journey toward success, and visually keeps you on track.

Do you remember the last time you sat down by yourself and committed to a specific goal? Do you remember the feelings you felt? Do you remember the emotion of anxiety because of the unknown? Do you remember the excitement because of possible success? These are all natural emotions when planning your goals. The key to moving this process forward is your passion. Place all of your negative emotions aside, dig deep down, and let passion be the driving force behind your goals.

The process of setting goals helps you choose where you want to go and gives you the blue-print on how to get there. Goals help you create long-term vision and short-term motivation. By knowing precisely what you want to achieve, you know where you have to concentrate your efforts. You'll also quickly spot the distractions that would otherwise get you off course.

Those with great vision are able to see that which is invisible to other people. The ability to continually visualize is vital to your success. Once vision breaks down, it's like driving a car in the dark with no headlights; it is impossible to find your destination.   So, remember that goals give you the road map and that vision provides the headlights.

Integrity is a characteristic that will live
through generations. How will you be
remembered?

Integrity

Integrity, integrity, integrity! When planning goals have the upmost integrity in every deci sion you make. Ever since I could walk I heard those words and I believe in a life of integrity. Stay true to yourself and your values no matter what! There is no dollar amount in this world that should shake your level of integrity. Make that commitment so intense that nothing can move you. It's not just saying you have integrity that makes that commitment so intense; it's how you act, react, and live your life when no one is looking. Trust me, along every path there is opportunity to compromise your values, but if you make up your mind beforehand, you will never have to think twice.

What a great feeling when you know your integrity is being tested and you don't budge. People will follow you, your kids will want to be like you, and you will leave a legacy behind by holding true to this simple principle. Remember, as I mentioned earlier, a way to measure your integrity is by how you act when no one is watching.

Focus is all about getting the mind to do what you want it to do.

Focus

Focus takes long-term vision and short-term motivation. Think about this for a minute. If you can master the mind to focus on these two efforts, nothing, and I mean nothing, should ever stop you from accomplishing your goals. When I think of focus, I think of one of the greatest athletes on the planet: Tiger Woods. What's interesting is that he is no different than Phil Mickelson, Vijay Singh, or Sergio Garcia when it comes to ability and talent. These men work in the same profession and are all considered professionals. So why is he consistently better?

I could write an entirely different book on why I believe Tiger is better than each of these individuals. Now obviously the principle of focus is only one piece to the puzzle. Nevertheless, all great ones have this in common! I challenge you to look into any profession in this world and find a top performer who says their individual focus has had little impact on their ability to succeed. I can assure you that while each answer may vary, each top performer will hold high value to the importance focus has had in their process to becoming the best.

Do you want to be great?

If you answered yes then focus! If you have never watched Tiger on a Saturday afternoon, I want you to spend 30 minutes whether you like golf or not and watch him play. Compare his focus to any other professional golfer on the planet. You will notice the vast difference in the way Tiger approaches the game, step by step and shot by shot.

Another example of focus that all of us will be able to relate to on some level is motherhood. Because this is such a special responsibility, I took the time to ask my wife, who is such an incredible mother, how focus has been such a big part of her life. Immediately after I asked her the question, she looked at me and smiled, and said, "I think about that word every day." There was a number of interesting comments that she made in regards to focus. The comment that stuck out the most was when she said that "in order to be successful as a mother, you have to learn to be selfless, and to give 100% all the time." What's interesting is that most people, myself included, spend our days focusing on something that most likely will immediately benefit ourself or someone else in a roundabout way. A mother's focus is purely to benefit the child. That's amazing to me!

Remember, there is no duty, profession, or goal in this world that is more important than the other. As a matter of fact, anyone who is able to put 100% focus to a task like a mother or like Tiger Woods, will always find joy and reward in what they do.

A non-arrogant attitude and self-pride gives
you the audacity to be a winner.

Attitude and Self Pride

Let's think about the above quote for a minute and understand what it means.

Self-pride: Make your goals clear, attainable and more importantly, take pride in accomplishing them. Don't be afraid to fail! My father always told me that "failure is the mother of all inventions." I believe that statement 110%! The feeling of failing literally makes me sick to my stomach; I absolutely hate it! Though I have been through it hundreds of times, and I know I will continue to fail because it's part of the process!

Attitude: I have always loved this word. As long as it is not an arrogant "attitude," I have never thought it was wrong. I want you to think of someone who carries themselves with "attitude" in a humble way. What do you think of this person? Do you like them? Do they have qualities you want?

When my father–in-law talks about my wife when she was a child, the word that he always uses to explain her is "attitude." What's interesting is that's the same word I would use to describe my wife years later. With "attitude" she walks, talks, and approaches life. If you were to ask me what I think her best qualities are then I would respond with caring, loving, and thoughtful. Does that sound like someone with "attitude?"

As you apply self-pride and attitude toward your short-term and long-term goals, you will feel a sense of inner security and outward strength and it will drive you through any obstacle that comes your way.

"Mediocrity is a choice not a place of birth."

Mediocrity

Remember that you are not born with predetermined or mediocre circumstances. You choose them. The mediocre are afraid to take chances. Try to forget about failing and take a risk. Without a doubt, along the process you will fail, but after you fail, get back up and do it again and again and again. I promise that you will find more joy in all the failure that comes your way than if you were to wallow in mediocrity because history has shown those who don't give up eventually succeed.

Separate yourself from the mediocre right now! You know who they are, and you know if you are. Strive for excellence and don't be one who never experiences victory or defeat. Take a chance on yourself! It's worth it, and so are you!

"Silence makes the mind loud."

Brainstorm

A while back I was struggling with life's challenges. They felt overwhelmingly heavy and I was having a difficult time focusing day-to-day. I approached a good friend for advice. He told me to take time out of my crazy life, to turn off the radio, the TV, and any other distraction and think, meditate and brainstorm. What powerful advice he gave me!

The mind is the greatest tool we have. If we don't fully utilize it, we are handicapping ourselves from the thought process necessary when building a plan.

So, when setting goals, or like me, when you're just attempting to pull yourself together, take time to brainstorm and think. Let your mind flow and dream. Visualize yourself achieving your goals. Before writing anything down, map out in your mind the pathway toward achieving your specific goal and picture the moment of triumph. Most importantly, make this a time of positive, quiet thoughts. Take out the negatives, the fears, and anything that would hold you back. Remember we gravitate to our dominant thought!

No wall is strong enough that it can't be broken.

Rocky Road

At times the road can get rocky, that's okay! Spend time revising your plan and adjusting your thought process so you stay on course. Never cut corners! If you are having trouble climbing a wall, plow through it! But understand that the course is always changing and you need to be flexible.

As you accept all the challenges in front of you, you will also learn to accept the rocky road you will most likely encounter. As you learn to accept the rocky road with every journey, find your own unique way to get through the rough times. For example, utilize family, friends, or even a spiritual leader to talk and share your struggles. You could also find a quiet place where you can think, write, or listen to music.

Whatever method you choose, remember this, hard times always pass and will always make you better in some way or another. Hang in there and don't give up.

Acknowledge good work and reward yourself often.

Reward Yourself

There is nothing in the world like a reward. I can't tell you how many times I have come home from work and my wife has made my favorite meal, dessert and set aside time to watch a favorite movie or watch a game. I don't know if I deserve it all the time, but one of my greatest goals in life is to be a great husband. I think she knows that and has taught me to stop and reward myself.

This concept should be applied as we attempt to pursue all passions and goals in our life. As you frequently stop and take time out of your daily routine to reward yourself, I promise you will feel more vivacity and your mind will have a greater sense of clarity.

Setting goals gives you purpose as you embark on any journey and begin living your passion.

Just to Get You Started

I am aware that the process of setting goals is fairly common in most lives. However, if you are not currently and consistently setting goals, here are some simple ideas to make it a habit:

1. Write down specific day-to-day goals at the beginning of each week.

2. Write down long-term goals.

3. Place your goals in a specific spot next to your bed and a second copy at work.

4. Each Sunday night review your goals; change the course if needed and re-commit.

5. Share your goals with family and friends.

Chapter 9

Practice

Trained reflex is achieved through practice.

Repetition

Practice is the fourth step in the Passion Cycle. I love this step because it reminds me of all the hard work, sweat, tears and love that is put into being successful. As you become accustomed to this principle, you will find strength, wisdom, and courage in your day-to-day activities.

Shooting 100 free throws, chipping 100 chips, catching 100 catches, or fielding 100 ground balls, will program your mind and body so that it reacts naturally for the 101st play during a game.

Is the world getting better?

The answer is 'yes.' This is because of prac-tice! We need to embrace practice as part of the challenge, and in order to keep up with the world, we need people who are willing to become experts.

Discipline is the act that helps you follow through.

Discipline

When our body and mind tells us "no," our discipline needs to say "yes." Practice is a continuous process, and will be an enormous part of your success with everything you do.

If ever the thought crosses your mind that there is no need to practice anymore, you are wrong! Create a routine in your life that keeps you disciplined. Understand that it is human nature to get extremely motivated initially, and then as time goes on, to fade away. When attempting to structure discipline in your life, learn to be realistic. Don't go overboard. Create a simple plan that will keep you on course, focused, and still give you time to breathe.

*Whatever "IT" is, learn to love "IT" and
"IT" will love you!*

Love "IT"

Remember this book is all about finding and
following your passion. As you follow your
passion by utilizing the powerful principles
in this book, your love will grow deeper and
deeper each day. Deep rooted love is a common driving force behind every relationship or
goal. Real genuine love for something can't
be broken.

There are many things in this life that catch our
eye, and few grab our heart. The unique things
that grab our hearts, we should pursue. I am
convinced that a big problem in this world today is that too many people pursue what they
want rather than what they love. Your options
may be few, but once you spend time pursuing the things you love, the art of practice will

become more enjoyable, more consistent, and a part of your life routine.

Ask anyone who has ever sacrificed anything
to become something if the blood sweat and
tears were worth it. I promise the response
will never change.

Challenge Yourself

Before you continue reading, I want you to take
15 minutes and go over these 3 tips:

First, without going overboard and crazy, commit the time necessary to practice. For example, if I were on a quest to perfect a sales pitch,
then one of the things I would do is practice
the sales pitch in my car on my way over to
work each day. Remember, the time commitment may vary with each situation. However,
do not cut corners. Be honest with yourself and
be smart. Utilize your time wisely.

Second, be patient and have fun! Not every goal
is going to be easy to practice, so don't forget
the simple words: patience and fun. This will
help you stay stress free. Stress in many ways

can hold people back from what they are trying to accomplish. So learn to laugh at yourself, and give yourself sufficient time.

Third, once a week, take sufficient time to evaluate yourself. This will allow you to overcome obstacles, and more importantly, it will provide a fresh start and a renewed sense of motivation. Also, ask yourself the simple question, "how was my practice?" Was it Poor, Mediocre, or Excellent? This exercise will give you an honest evaluation and prepare you for weeks to come.

Chapter 10

Self
Talk

Your inner thought will determine greatly who you are.

Karate Kid

Self-Talk is the fifth step in the Passion Cycle. This step is the key, because our mind is in control of our actions. By communicating positive affirmations you will learn to walk with poise, and also understand the power you hold within yourself. In this chapter, I will show you two examples of why self-talk is so powerful each and every day we live. One story is fictional and the other real life.

Who is the Karate Kid? I'm going to start out by saying what we all thought about Daniel LaRusso years ago for the first time when we watched the Karate Kid . . ."That's one skinny little wimp!" Now, what made that show great was that by the end of the show Daniel not only believed he wasn't a wimp, but he believed that he was tougher than everyone else.

This chapter will reveal secrets to how Daniel became a champ. One specific part in the movie that impressed me was toward the end when Daniel had to fight some of the best fighters in the final tournament, including Johnny of the Cobra Kai. During this segment, as it leads up to the final fight, a song comes on that you may remember. To me the lyrics have been clear ever since I was a child when I saw this movie for the first time. To this day it does two things; it makes me laugh and motivates me to be better. Please sing along if you remember the words:

"Nothing's gonna ever keep you down, you're the best around . . ."

And they repeat those words numerous times throughout the song. I want you to take a minute and think about those words:

"Nothing's gonna ever keep you down, you're the best around . . ."

Now I want you to say this out loud no matter where you are, and say it like you mean it! "Nothing's gonna ever keep me down, I'm the best around . . ."

Did you do it? That's okay if you didn't. What I really want is that you ingrain this thought in your head and believe it with everything you've got, because you are the best and never ever let anyone bring you down!

The idle mind is a dangerous mind that can do no good.

The Idle Mind

Learn to think about something! People gravitate to their dominant thought. So, if your dominant thought is to succeed, guess what? You will probably succeed. If your thought is failure you will probably fail. This is a concept my father has explained and taught to me hundreds of times throughout my life, and you know what, it's absolutely true!

Since your mind will get tired and idol, you need to find something to fill in the gaps! I like the saying, "you can tell who someone really is by what they think about when they don't have to think."

That's scary for some people! So, what do you think about when you don't have to think? Is it a good thought? Is it bad? Is it productive or dangerous? In the upcoming pages, I will give you some ideas to always keep your mind moving in the right direction.

*A mind that is mastered is one that chooses
what it wants to hear and how it wants to
think.*

K.I.S.S.

Have you ever heard the phrase K.I.S.S?

Keep. It. Simple. Stupid.   That is a phrase
that has been used for years in sales trainings
throughout the world, and I love it! Don't com-
plicate your mind; keep it simple! You have
two categories that will help control your mind:
Dominant thoughts and filler thoughts.

In this book, we spend the majority of the time
talking about the dominant thoughts. Understand that the key to always maintaining positive dominant thoughts is learning how to fill
in the gaps where you don't have to think, with
optimistic positive thoughts.

One way to fill in the gaps is through positive

affirmation.   Affirmations are positive state-ments of a desired goal. These are usually goals that are realistic and attainable.   The key is to repeat the goal over and over again.   By do-ing so you open up the mind to new thoughts and create a pathway toward achieving it. A big part of affirmation is learning to repeat it aloud, and more importantly, that you say it with pas-sion and conviction.   However, simply saying the words bears no consequence unless you put some emotions behind them.

Getting to the top from the bottom is a choice
accompanied with action.

The Best Salesman

I have a good friend who I have worked with for years. I would consider him a very talented high class individual, but in sales he was always in the middle of the pack. One Monday he walked into work and proclaimed to me that this week amongst sixty salesmen he was going to be at the top of the chart. I gladly pushed him to the challenge but deep down I wondered how he would do it up against some of the best salesman in the state.

After day one, he was far ahead of the pack. I was quite surprised that after day two he was so far ahead that he was on his way to surpass all our sales records. In the end, he demolished our records and placed himself as the best salesperson in the office. I sat down with him on Friday afternoon and asked him what he did different than before. He said it was simple. Before the week began he started telling himself, "I am the best salesman in our office." He continued doing this every night before he went to bed, when he woke up, and as he drove into the office. Incredibly, it is the simple principle of positive affirmation combined with belief that can take you to places you may never have imagined. I don't think until that week he ever thought he was the best salesperson in the office, but in one week he placed himself in a new category personally and in the eyes of a whole organization. That's incredible to me!

So what stops you from always applying this principle each day?

The application of positive self-talk is a straightforward and easy concept. Anybody who wants to apply this principle could do it in just minutes every day. More importantly, just like the story of my friend, you can reach miraculous results.

Positive self-talk, in its simplest meaning, is the act of removing negative thoughts and emotions from one's mind.

Positive affirmations:

I am a good person.

I am a happy person.

I am honest.

I am a successful person.

I am courageous.

I am a good friend.

I am a hard worker.

I am loyal.

I am strong.

I am the best.

Laughter breeds optimism.

Optimistic People

I love positive people! Unfortunately, this world is full of so many negative people--don't be one of them! Surround yourself with positive, passionate, happy people that make you feel good. If, by chance, you absolutely have to associate with someone negative, always do two things. First, find the good in them. It's easy to place judgment on people if all you see are their negatives. Second, always, always be positive around them. Never join in on the negativity. Remember, positive people are contagious! Trust me, within time you will rub off on them.

Ultimately, our minds should be a place of continual peace. At night, when you put your head down to rest, you should try to resolve all negative thoughts and enjoy the beauty of sleep. This will create optimism and help start each day refreshed.

Chapter 11

Go
Get
"IT"

Patience helps perfect the task at hand.

Go Get "IT"

"Go Get It." This is the sixth and last step in the Passion Cycle. I love this step because it gives you a sense of invincibility. I hope you can feel my energy through this book, particularly at this point. Please understand that I have no doubt that you can achieve anything in this world that you want to. Now, all you have to do is "Go Get It"!

Once you have set your eyes on something, Go Get "It!" Execute your plan and carry it out to perfection. Your plan will take much pressure off you as you go through the inevitable ups and downs. Regularly study your plan and always have a mental visualization of it.

Be patient with yourself and take the time necessary to get where you are going. I've never found it beneficial to speed to a destination. All you'll gain is a quick rush and possible disaster. Enjoy the scenery and only accelerate when it's necessary. But no matter what level of speed you choose, Go Get "It" and don't let anyone get in your way.

Ignite the fire within you.

On Fire

When was the last time you ignited the fire within you?

How did that feel?

There is no feeling in the world like being on fire. If you feel it, then spread it, share it and capitalize on it.

By this time, you should be tasting victory. If you can make it to this point with a specific desire or passion, you are almost there. Now it's a matter of not letting anyone get in your way. Learn at this point to put your foot on the pedal and accelerate. If you have ever accelerated while driving a car you understand what it feels like. This same thrill is available to those who don't give up.

It is funny that human nature makes people want to slow down once you know you have almost won. Learn to never let up, especially when the feeling of triumph is near.

Winning is an irreplaceable thrill.

Walking Like a Winner

Do you walk and talk like a winner? I do not care what your circumstances are; rich or poor, thin or fat, small or tall—walk like you have won, talk like you have won, and make sure when people meet you they know you are a winner. I promise you that if you practice being a winner in every aspect of your life, you will find yourself winning more often than not. No matter how many times you've lost or failed, continue walking like a winner. I assure you that victory will always be just around the corner.

Winners are winners no matter what. I can take someone who believes they are a winner, put them in a foreign scenario and tell them to win. Within time, I guarantee they would win.

We always hear the cliché that champions are not born, they are made. I believe that 100%. I have never spoken with anyone in my life that cannot be made a winner. No one! If the thought had ever crept into your mind that you are a loser or that you cannot do something you have set out to do, you are wrong!

When your back is to the wall it is the response and reaction that largely defines your character.

Fight or Flight

Fight or flight is a common term used when faced with a physical or mental confrontation.

I am assuming we have all seen The Christmas Story. If not, this movie is about a young boy who's biggest Christmas wish from Santa was to get a Red Rider BB gun. Ralphy came across many obstacles in this movie. One was the bully of the neighborhood. One snowy afternoon as he was walking with his friends, he had to make a choice when he found the bully pushing him around, taunting him to fight. Do I cry and run off looking for mom or do I take a shot at this bully, win, lose, or draw? Do you remember what little Ralphy did? He took a shot and fought, and look what happened. As we all know he won the fight! Now, I don't give this example to promote fighting. That will not get you anywhere. In spite of this, think of a time when you have felt your back to the wall mentally or physically and you had nowhere to go. What was your instinct? Was it fight or flight? If you said fight, good for you! If you said flight that is okay. However, starting today I want you to fight!

In order to fully understand this behavior you first need to recognize that when placed in a situation like this, your nerves, your blood pressure, your mind, and your heart rate will all change. So, the key to learning how to fight is understanding and recognizing these behaviors and then learning how to control them in moments of challenge or confrontation. Once you understand this, you can make a decision to fight. If that fails like it did for Ralphy from The Christmas Story, then just fight. I think you will be surprised at the outcome!

Here are a few tips when faced in common Fight or Flight situations:

•   Breathe calmly in through your nose and out through your mouth

- Think quickly and rationally

- Be logical when you speak

- Listen carefully

- Speak strong and clearly

- Make direct eye contact

- Smile, it will loosen up your body

The light bulb was created to shed light--and so were people.

The "Zone"

During the 90's, we were all a witness to the greatest basketball player to ever live, Michael Jordan. On numerous occasions, we witnessed him get in the zone as he raised himself and his team to a higher level in order to win an important game. He was the epitome of the zone, and that is a big reason why he is the greatest basketball player to ever live.

The zone is the highest level of focus and performance. Fortunately, it can be used in all situations of life, not just sports. You could be a father, mother, salesman, accountant, teacher, student, bus driver, or a contractor. Whatever the situation is, getting in the zone is vital to success. The zone takes hard work and is typically unpredictable when it comes.

Flipping the switch is different than the zone in that it is predictable energy that can be turned on and off. Most people operate life's energy on 50-100%. We bounce in and out of high points and low points each and every day. The key is learning how to flip the switch to 110% and operate at a higher level than everyone else around you. Remember the importance of saving energy when you turn off a light switch. So too, you must flip your inner switch to preserve the energy that you have. A light bulb that is left on too long will eventually burn out, much like our bodies will burn out if we don't learn to turn it on and off.

*Self-belief is about standing aside yourself
and trusting who you are.*

Believe in Yourself

Believe in yourself. To be great, believe in your unique talents that you have been given. Never let anyone tear down the inner belief inside you. More importantly, don't allow yourself to tear down the inner belief inside you. If you ever feel this belief inside you slipping away, quickly take the time and find someone you trust to talk! Yes, talk. Talking to someone you trust is one of the best ways to build back your self-belief. Even more importantly than talking to a friend, do not forget to be honest to that friend because if you are genuine they will be genuine. They will help you take a look from the outside in.

Take chances and be someone different.

Gain a reputation for doing the impossible. Simply put, the impossible is typically any given challenge that people do not want to do. Always take the challenge, don't be afraid! Set yourself apart as someone always willing to do the impossible, and believe in yourself that you can.

Be the one who initiates excitement, laughter and fun.

Have Fun!

If the above quote is the last thing you remember in this book that is okay.   Do not forget to have fun. Look at the glass half-full. See the positive. Laugh when times get hard. Play when you want to play, and smile when you do not want to smile. There is nothing in the world like being around people who like to have fun. This chapter is so important to the Passion Cycle because it teaches you how to finish. The most important message to understand from this process is to learn how to stop at times during the heat of battle and HAVE FUN!

Chapter 12

Accountability

Be who you say you are, and live up to the
light you have been given.

Be True to Yourself

As you strive to achieve greatness through the
Passion Cycle, I want you to be true to yourself
and be accountable to the person that you are.
The six principles you have just learned will be
the key to each goal you attempt to achieve. I
love life and love watching people succeed. I
hope this last chapter cements passion in your
soul and helps hold you accountable to the person you are.

Two years ago, a close friend of mine chal-
lenged me to write a personal mission statement. I have to admit, it took months to finally
finish, though I finally did it mainly because my
friend was very persistent. I am grateful that he
pushed me. Since I have finished, I have modi-
fied it many times, referred back to it often, and

held true to the values and standards that I envision for myself.

Holding yourself accountable on paper and sharing your dreams with individuals you care about are important elements to self-accountability. Generally, in life, I have been fairly conservative with sharing my life's challenges, standards and passions. Years ago, someone told me that in order to grow closer to people you need to share your weaknesses and goals. I have always used that method of communication with close friends and it has been extremely important with close relationships I want to cultivate. The most challenging part about writing a book is opening up your life to everyone. But since I have finished this book, I believe I have become a better person and communicator to those around me.

I want to share with you my personal mission statement. Then, I want to challenge each one of you to take the time and write a personal mission statement of your own. Remember to share it with people, add to it and hold true to your values.

Stand up for what you believe in no matter what the circumstances are.

Sample Mission Statement

The following is my personal mission statement. The success that I have in life will be balanced around four words: Passion, Pride, Team, and Vision. These have such a profound meaning to me.

Passion: It is very important that I continue being a passionate person and have passion with everything I do. It starts with my marriage, then my family which needs to be the root of my passion. Passion is a natural gift I have been given, and I will exert it and like a wild fire try to help people feel the passion I have for life.

Pride: I will take pride in my mind for the mind is the most powerful tool we have been given; it controls all of our actions. I will take pride in my integrity, my loyalty, and my honesty in everything I do. I will learn, practice, and study because we have been given infinite ability to attain knowledge. I will work hard and take pride in being the best. I will strive to be humble, and most of all, take pride in serving others.

Team: there is no I in team. More things can and will be accomplished if I learn to work as a team in everything I do. I will learn to become a better listener, a better communicator, and to have a better sense of humor, because this is the foundation of a team. I will learn to lead a team and to follow a team. I will not seek out recognition, I will give it. The greatest of all teams is the team I develop with my wife, and I will work every day to make our team as solid as a rock in every aspect.

Vision: To have vision you need to understand where you are going and have the ability not to let anyone stop you. I will learn to be a thinker. I will learn to build maps and blueprints to where I am going. I will learn to hold more will, more determination, and more faith as I head on each journey of life.

All the happiness you will ever find in life is
found inside of you.

Final Thought

Say what you want to say, do what you want to do, and be who you want to be. How beautiful it is to be alive today, to have an active mind, and the ability to do what we want to do. Nobody can take that away from us. Regardless of your situation, learn to be bold and live your life without fear. With that in mind, whatever "IT" is, go get "IT"! And let passion guide you as you build "IT".

If you would like more guidance or instruction
on following your passion please visit:

www.builditonpassion.com

or contact Tony via email at:

builditonpassion@hotmail.com